end of the rainbow

Komal Jain

BookLeaf Publishing

India | USA | UK

Presentation by *BookLeaf Publishing*

Web: www.bookleafpub.com

E-mail: info@bookleafpub.com

ISBN: 9789363301764

First edition 2024

This book is for -

*Jyoti, my mom - who believed I would be a
great writer one day*

*Navin, my dad - who thinks his daughter can do
anything*

*Nehal, my sister - who is my number-one
cheerleader*

*Rishi, my husband - who thinks I am a great
writer already*

*Abhishek and Jyoti, my friends - who have
always encouraged my writing*

I love you all!

ACKNOWLEDGEMENT

My writing is inspired by almost everyone I have ever met in my life - both good and bad. You have all given me a perspective, a topic, and motivation, so thank you!

To all those who thought I had a bit of talent to write, for always encouraging me to keep this passion ignited. Thank you! You made this possible!

To my friends, who either really liked my work, or faked liking it, I have always appreciated your support!

To Mom, Dad, sister, and husband, my biggest fans and critics - thank you for everything!

And last, but not the least, I want to thank myself - for not giving up on my love for writing, and marching on!

PREFACE

When I came across the opportunity to write this book, I was going through a very tumultuous time. This book has given me a perfect outlet for my creativity and emotions and has helped me see the good on bad days.

I have converted my raw emotions into poems.

I hope you like my work, for I have poured my heart into these cute little poems!

before you say goodnight

when things seem dark
in the middle of the night
all you see is darkness
nothing else in sight
now seems like forever
the surroundings are becoming tight
fear is taking over
you don't know how to fight
when it feels like the end
before you say g'night
think, is it really so dark
or did you forget to turn on the light

splitter splatter

raining by the window
couch, tea, a book in hand
splitter-splatter, splitter-splatter
this setting feels so grand
forget your worries for a while
grief, regret, or deep old sorrow
splitter-splatter, splitter-splatter
postpone that worry for tomorrow
take a break from worry
read the book, sip the tea
splitter-splatter, splitter-splatter
all the way to glory

you

there is a small garden
in my heart
where I grow flowers
for you
there is a pocket
in my wallet
where i keep a picture
of you
there is a small page
in my notebook
where I write
i love you
there is a big part
of my life
which belongs
to you

in my wildest dreams

in my wildest dreams, i see a routine life
studying for an exam, watching tv
having some dinner, extra gravy
going for a walk, gossip galore
everyone so happy, beaming and more

in my wildest dreams, i feel at home
lazying on the couch, reading a book
thinking all the time, what to cook
while eating chips and fries and cake
so tired—let's take a break!

drafts

have you ever
messaged someone while crying
mist clouding your eyes
so hard you are trying
you write your heart out
in a single paragraph
and yet you delete it
and save it to your drafts

you open that draft
years later, and realise
how far you have come
after so many tries
a hint of a smile, a distant memory
something had fallen while you typed
your favourite bookend
you can still hear the sound
of the mental clunk, and think to yourself
how much you had wanted to hit send

today

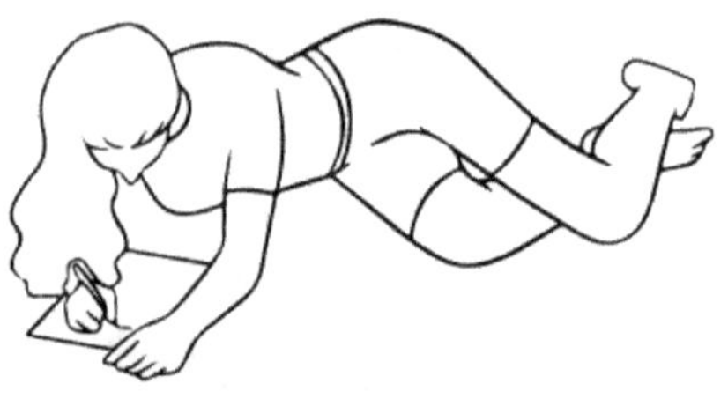

do you remember how much
you wanted what you have
in this present moment
of happiness and joy
wishes, hopes, and prayers
all came together, and
granted you this life, so
take a moment and enjoy

don't think about tomorrow
just live in the present
be thankful and grateful
keep your worries at bay
your life, your family
your friends, your health
bask in the glory
of this hard-earned today!

flipside

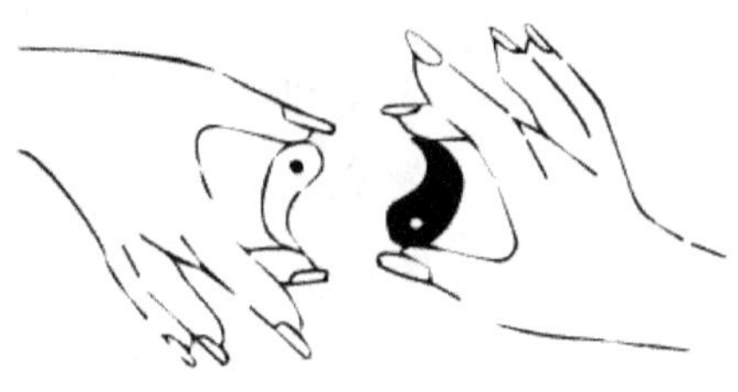

pesky relatives,
rude neighbors,
rowdy manager,
arrogant co-workers
But
loving sisters,
loyal pets,
loyal partner,
as good as it gets

we often get distracted
by all the bad things
while our treasurers
hide in plain sight
negativity takes the lead
becomes more important
but try to remember
there is always a flipside

chaos is me

in the midst of chaos
can you see me
trembling, wounded, scared
can you hear me
shouting, crying, wailing
can you feel me
upset, unwell, unhinged

you know what
you cannot
for i hide in plain sight
i hide my fears with a smile
my darkness with a twinkle of the eye
my tears with laughs
my wounds with fancy marks

in the midst of chaos
you cannot see me
because guess what
chaos is me

fall apart

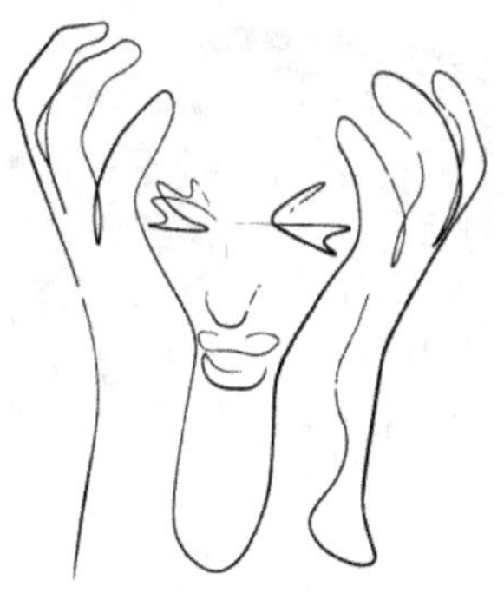

fall apart if you must
honour your feelings
honour your emotions
for if you don't
you will fall apart
regardless
but then, you will not be able to
piece yourself back up
and then, you will become
nothing but a mess

reading

what whetstones are for swords
our mind gets from words
if you read
never stop
if you don't
give it a shot

if you think you don't like reading, look—
you haven't yet found the perfect book
a loyal friend
portable magic
an ever-giving gift
an epic classic

so pick up that book
you did? see how little that took
to hold such imagination
in your hands
now let yourself immerse
in words, beauty, and magical lands

why should i change

why should i change
are you the same?
why is it always my fault
when all you do is blame
 faulting me for things so fickle
so small, so unimportant
in the sea of love, a tiny trickle

why should i change
when you fell in love
with you i was
not who i might have
become through your expectations,
your anger, so unimportant
in the sea of love, a big salvation

one morning

one morning, you will breathe
like you used to
with peace and comfort
watching the morning dew

one morning, you will feel
like you used to
safe and happy
this was long overdue

one morning, you will smile
like you used to
feeling thankful and grateful
for the difficulties you overgrew

let this morning be today
when you feel this way
take a deep breath
relax and feel safe
smile with your eyes
because
only one person can make this true—
only you can get to be you

aching heart

left shoulder
heavy with memories
right shoulder
heavy with letting go
chest in between,
trying to remain calm
decides against a tug-of-war
just keeps moving on and on,
with an aching heart, next door

happiness

if you want to find happiness
first, find gratitude
if you want to feel joyful
it's all in your attitude

without being thankful
for what you have
you cannot feel happy
but just have a few dry laughs

say thank you to the Universe
every chance you get
and see how quickly
happiness is all you get

all a woman wants

all a woman wants
is the freedom to be
her authentic self
no facades, nothing wannabe

all a woman wants
is the freedom to become
who she aspires, and not what's
expected by her dad and mum

all a woman wants
is the freedom to fade
to rest and keep aside
the oh-so-heavy "expectations" weight

all a woman wants
is the freedom to fail
sometimes, like everyone,
without any consequences or trail

if a woman can get freedom
she will soar like a bird
she will conquer the skies
and rule the mighty world

stranger

why is it always
that it takes a stranger
to tell us
how important we are

to give us the validation
we seek everywhere
to show us how easy
it is to care

to make us believe
in all our prayers
why is it always
that it takes a stranger

the night we met

take me back to the night we met
starry skies
starry eyes
just one glance and everything was set

it was a simple day, yet
butterflies were moonstruck
butterflies in the stomach
a night that we'll never forget

just like in movies, during sunset
nervous walks
nervous talks
holding hands, our silhouettes

the one i am becoming

let me fall
if i must fall
the one i am becoming will catch me

let me fail
if i must fail
the one i am becoming will patch me

let me break
if i must break
the one i am becoming will reattach me

for who i am becoming
is who i was
is who i am
and who i will be
for who i am becoming
is wiser
is happier
is braver
and always there for me

to me

to the girl i was
i love you!
to the woman i am
i adore you!
to the lady i am becoming
i am proud of you!

healing

that relief after healing
from what you are healing now
will be the most magical breath
full of life and how

those tears after healing
from what you are healing now
will be drops of happy gold
you made it, somehow

that prayer after healing
from what you are healing now
will be full of gratitude
the prayer, always, was no one but thou

marriage

that's the funny thing
about marriage
you fall in love
with this person
who is extraordinary
and over time
they begin to seem
so ordinary

it's important to remember
they are still your chosen one
your partner in crime
your best friend
your partner *extraordinaire*
the love of your life
they are
anything but *ordinaire*